The Young Geographer Investigates

Deserts

Terry Jennings

Oxford University Press

Oxford University Press, Walton Street, Oxford OX2 6DP

Oxford   New York   Toronto
Delhi   Bombay   Calcutta   Madras   Karachi
Petaling Jaya   Singapore   Hong Kong   Tokyo
Nairobi   Dar es Salaam   Cape Town
Melbourne   Auckland

and associated companies in
Berlin   Ibadan

Oxford is a trade mark of Oxford University Press

ISBN 0 19 917071 1 (Paperback)
First published 1986
Reprinted 1988, 1989, 1990

ISBN 0 19 917077 0 (Hardback)
First published 1986
Reprinted 1988, 1990

© Terry Jennings

Typeset in Great Britain by
Tradespools Ltd., Frome, Somerset
Printed in Hong Kong

Acknowledgements

The publishers would like to thank the following for permission to reproduce transparencies:

Alastair Scott: p. 5 (bottom right); Aspect Picture Library: p. 33 (bottom right),
p. 4 (bottom), p. 6 (top), p. 37 (top), p. 7 (top), p. 16 (centre left), p. 26 (right),
p. 26 (left), p. 31 (centre left); Camerapix Hutchison Library: p. 12 (bottom);
CHL/David Bartholomew: p. 8 (left); CHL/Sara Errington: p. 12 (centre), p. 29
(centre), p. 38 (centre right); CHL/David Simpson: p. 16 (right); CHL/Val &
Alan Wilkinson: p. 28 (top); CHL/Piers Hammick: p. 30 (centre); CHL/Melanie
Friend: p. 34 (bottom right); CHL/Chris Parker: p. 34 (right); CHL/Brian
Moser: p. 35 (top and bottom left), p. 39 (top left); CHL/John Wright: p. 46;
Bruce Coleman Limited/Jan Taylor: p. 5 (bottom left); Coleman/Norman
Myers: p. 7 (bottom right); Coleman/John Shaw: p. 8 (top right); Coleman/
Stephen Krasemann: p. 8 (centre right); Coleman/Rod Williams: p. 9 (top
right); Coleman/M.P.L. Fogden: p. 9 (bottom left), p. 10 (inset); Coleman/
B & C Calhoun: p. 10, p. 36 (centre right); Coleman/Carol Hughes: p. 14
(centre), p. 17 (bottom), cover; Coleman/Rod Borland: p. 16 (bottom left);
Coleman/Leonard Lee Rue: p. 30 (bottom); Coleman/Simon Trevor: p. 31
(bottom); Coleman/Jen & Des Bartlett: p. 32 (top); Coleman/Gerald Cubitt:
p. 38 (top); Tor Eigeland: p. 27 (bottom right); Robert Estall: p. 39 (right); Sally
and Richard Greenhill: p. 11 (top); Susan Griggs/Victor Englebert: p. 5 (top
right); Griggs/Tor Eigeland: p. 27 (bottom left); Griggs/Anthony Howarth:
p. 38 (bottom right); Robert Harding Picture Library: p. 11 (bottom), p. 32
(centre right), p. 36 (left); Harding/Ian Griffiths: p. 5 (top left); Harding/Jon
Gardey: p. 11 (centre); Harding/Carol Jopp: p. 30 (top); Harding/G & P
Corrigan: p. 39 (centre left); Alan Hutchison: p. 31 (centre right); Hilly Janes:
p. 33 (left); Terry Jennings: p. 4 (top), p. 7 (bottom left), p. 9 (bottom right),
p. 22 (inset), p. 23, p. 27 (top), p. 28 (centre), p. 29 (top); Tony Morrison: p. 14
(top), p. 29 (bottom), p. 34 (top and bottom left), p. 38 (left); Natural Science
Photos: p. 35 (bottom right); Oxford Scientific Films/J.A.L. Cooke: p. 9 (centre
left), Spectrum Colour Library: p. 15, p. 17 (top), p. 36 (bottom right); John
Topham Picture Library: p. 32 (centre left), p. 33 (top right); US Department of
Agriculture/Ray Jackson

Illustrated by Stephen Cocking Gary Hincks Peter Joyce Ed McLachlan
Ben Manchipp Bernard Robinson (Tudor Art Studio)

Contents

Deserts 4
Where are the world's deserts? 5
Hot deserts 6
Plants in the desert 7
Baobab trees and cacti 8
Wild animals in the desert 9
More desert animals 10
Camels 11
Arabian and bactrian camels 12
Why deserts are formed 13
More reasons why deserts are
    formed 14
Man-made deserts 15
Water in the desert 16
The effects of the desert weather 17
Do you remember? 18
Things to do 19
Things to find out 25
Oases 26
People in the desert 27
The Sahara desert 28
Date palms 29
The Kalahari desert 30
Kalahari Bushmen 31
The Australian desert 32
Australian Aborigines 33
The Atacama desert 34
The Gobi desert 35
The Great American desert 36
The desert long ago 37
Wealth in the desert 38
Planting the desert 39
Do you remember? 40
Things to do 41
Things to find out 46
Glossary 47
Index 48

Deserts

An oasis near Douz, in Tunisia

A cold desert scene near Thule in Greenland

Deserts are dry lands where very little rain falls and where few plants can grow. More than one-seventh of the land on Earth is taken up by desert. Scientists usually say that a piece of ground is a desert if an average of less than 25 centimetres of rain falls each year. The rain does not fall evenly throughout the year. It usually falls in heavy storms.

Really there are two kinds of desert. One is very cold. Such cold deserts are found in the Arctic and Antarctic regions of the world. Here the ground is covered with ice and snow for all or most of the year. In these cold deserts little rain falls and few plants are able to grow. The other kind is the hot desert. Hot deserts are mostly sunny and very dry. It is these hot deserts which are described in this book. Cold deserts are described in another book in this series called *Polar Regions*.

4

Where are the world's deserts?

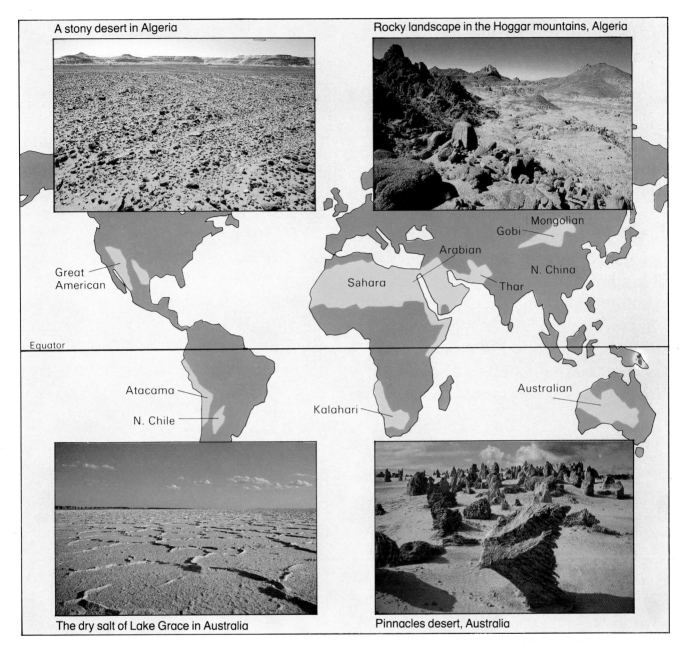

A stony desert in Algeria

Rocky landscape in the Hoggar mountains, Algeria

Great American

Sahara

Arabian

Gobi

Mongolian

N. China

Thar

Equator

Atacama

N. Chile

Kalahari

Australian

The dry salt of Lake Grace in Australia

Pinnacles desert, Australia

The map shows where the great deserts of the world are found. As you can see, there are deserts in Africa, Asia, Australia, North America and South America.

We usually think of deserts as being sandy. Here the wind has blown the sand into hills called sand-dunes.

But not all deserts are sandy. In most, the wind has blown the sand away leaving pebbles or even bare rock. In some deserts shallow lakes form after rain. These dry up in the sun leaving only a flat layer of glistening salt. Elsewhere there are mountains and steep rocky slopes. In places the rocks have beautiful shapes.

Hot deserts

Hot deserts are the driest places on Earth. In some there may be no rain for several years. During the day it is usually sunny, scorching hot and dry. It may be so hot that you could fry an egg on the sand or rocks. But at night it can be bitterly cold in the desert. It may be so cold that it freezes. The reason for these big differences in temperature is that there are no clouds in desert areas.

In most parts of the world, clouds stop some of the sun's rays from reaching the Earth. And so the Earth does not get too hot. At night when the sun is not shining the Earth cools down. But clouds stop some of the heat from escaping high into the air.

A stony desert in Libya

However, in deserts there are few clouds to stop the sun's rays heating the ground during the day. And so the ground becomes very hot. At night there are no clouds to stop the heat escaping. And so the desert cools very quickly.

At night the clouds hold the warm air down   Hot air deflected

Temperate Woodland

The cloudless desert sky lets heat escape   Hot air rising

Desert

Plants in the desert

All plants need light and air. They also need water. But it is hard for desert plants to get enough water to survive. Desert plants have developed ways to make use of every drop of water. We say they have adapted to these dry places.

There may be no plants in the desert for many months or even years. But scattered in the sand are the seeds of the plants that flowered the last time it rained. When it rains again these seeds suddenly start to grow. Within a few days the desert is covered with a carpet of flowers. After a few days or weeks, the flowers shrivel as the desert dries out. The flowers die, but the plants drop their seeds to wait for the next rain.

It may be dry on the surface of the desert, but there is often water deep underground. Some desert plants have long roots to reach this water. The roots of the acacia tree may go down 30 metres or more to reach water. The

Spring in the Namaqualand desert, South Africa

mesquite bush of the North American deserts sends its roots down to a depth of 50 metres. In the driest period the trees may lose their leaves.

Many desert plants have leaves with thick waterproof skins. They have leaf pores that can be tightly shut. This helps to stop water evaporating from the plant.

An acacia tree

Mesquite bush in Death Valley, California, USA

Baobab trees and cacti

A baobab tree

Saguaro cacti in Arizona

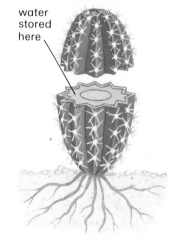

water stored here

A typical cactus stores water inside

The stem and spines of a prickly pear cactus

Some desert plants survive by storing water. The cacti can do this. They grow in the American deserts. A cactus stores water in its thick stem. Its roots spread far and wide, but only just below the surface of the ground. When it rains, the cactus roots can take in the water before it soaks away. The roots can also take up the dew which forms on the cold ground at night.

After a fall of rain the stem of a cactus may be filled with water. The plant then begins to live on the water it has stored. As it uses up the water, the stem of the cactus gradually shrivels. It gets thinner and thinner until the next rain comes. To stop water evaporating, the leaves of most cacti plants have been reduced to thorny spines. These spines protect the cactus from being eaten by animals.

Baobab or bottle trees grow in the Kalahari and Australian deserts. The barrel-shaped trunk of a baobab tree can be as much as 10 metres in diameter. The tree looks as if it has been planted upside down. As it gets older, it becomes hollow inside, and water is stored in this hollow trunk. Over 1000 litres have been found in a single trunk. Thirsty travellers in the desert can often obtain water from the baobab tree or cacti.

Wild animals in the desert

Few animals live in the desert because there is little water. Those animals which do live in the desert have to make do with very little water. Many of them never drink at all. They get the water they need from the desert plants and other foods they eat.

All the desert animals have to find ways to keep cool. Many of them come out only at night to feed. During the day they hide in burrows or under rocks where it is cool.

One of the most common animals in the Sahara desert is the jerboa. It is often called the desert rat. The jerboa is famous for being a good jumper. It spends much of its life underground away from the sun. The jerboa plugs the entrance of its burrow during the day to keep the hot air out. The

A leopard gecko in the shade of a rock

kangaroo rat of California is very similar in appearance to the jerboa. It has a similar way of life.

The gerbils we keep as pets were originally desert animals. They came from the sandy deserts of Mongolia and northern China.

A jerboa

The wild gerbil feeds at night

The kangaroo rat

More desert animals

An alert kit fox

The scorpion has a deadly sting in its tail

Animals which live in deserts need to have good sight and hearing. Those which eat smaller animals need good sight and hearing to catch their prey. Animals which eat plants often have to travel long distances to find their food. They must always be alert if they are to avoid being eaten.

Many desert animals have large ears. Desert hares have much larger ears than those of hares which live elsewhere. The kit fox of the North American desert also has large ears.

So does the tiny fennec fox of the Sahara desert. Desert animals lose a lot of heat through their large ears. The ears act like radiators. In this way their ears help the animals to stay cool.

One of the commonest small desert animals is the scorpion. Scorpions only come out at night. During the day they hide under rocks or in deep burrows. Scorpions feed mainly on insects which they kill with the sting in their tail.

Camels

Camels are probably the best known desert animals. These large animals have humps on their backs. The camel's toes are joined together by a fleshy pad which acts like a snow-shoe. It stops the camel from sinking in the soft sand. Camel fur traps a layer of air. This helps to keep the body cool during the day and warm at night. Camels have long eyelashes to protect their eyes from the sand. Their nostrils can be closed to keep the sand out.

The camel can run at a speed of about 8 to 10 kilometres an hour. Camels are used to carry loads across the desert. They are often called 'ships of the desert'. A long line of camels is called a camel train or a caravan. People also need camels for meat and their hides.

Camels have special eyelashes and nostrils

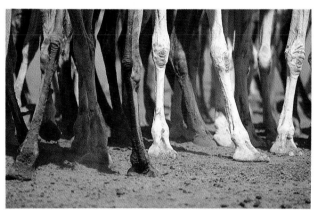
Broad feet help camels to stand firm

A camel train in the Sahara desert

Arabian and bactrian camels

One hump or two?

There are two kinds of camel. The Arabian camel or dromedary is found in the Middle East, India and North Africa. It has a single hump. The other kind of camel is the bactrian. This has two humps. The bactrian lives in the deserts of central Asia where the winters are cold. It is smaller than the dromedary and has a longer, darker winter coat and short legs.

Dromedaries drinking

A baby dromedary and its parents

A camel can go a long time without water. It can lose about one-third of the weight of its body and still live. Then when the camel does find water it can drink 115 litres or more in a few minutes.

Many people think that a camel stores water in its hump or stomach. This is not true. The camel's hump contains fat. This fat acts as a food store. It enables the camel to go many days without food.

Why deserts are formed

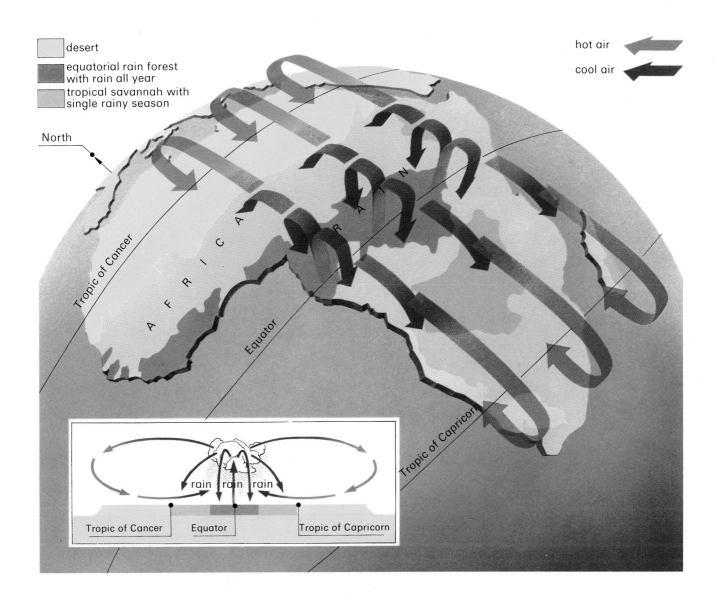

desert

equatorial rain forest
with rain all year

tropical savannah with
single rainy season

hot air

cool air

North

Tropic of Cancer

A F R I C A

Equator

R A I N

Tropic of Capricorn

rain rain rain

Tropic of Cancer   Equator   Tropic of Capricorn

Deserts are usually formed because of a lack of rain. But the reason for the lack of rain is not always the same.

If you look at the map on page 5, you will see that the large deserts are all about the same distance north or south of the Equator. When air is heated over the Equator it rises up. The warm, moist air passes high over the deserts. Eventually it cools and the water vapour in the clouds falls as heavy rain over the tropical forests.

The large masses of air move down towards the Earth again. But they are now dry. The dry winds blow across the regions where deserts are found, and back towards the Equator. The winds pick up moisture from the seas, lakes and rivers as they pass along. Because the winds are dry as they pass over the deserts there are no clouds or rain. And the sun's heat beats down upon the dry Earth below.

More reasons why deserts are formed

Some other areas are deserts because they are so far from the sea. Usually places near the sea are warmer than those inland. As a result, when warm, moist winds blow inland, they cool and lose their moisture, as rain, on the way. When the winds reach places far inland they are dry. The Gobi desert is so far inland that the winds have lost all their moisture long before they get there.

But some deserts are near to the sea. The Atacama desert in South America is near to the sea. It is a desert because the wind blows from the land to the sea. The wind has no chance to pick up moisture while it blows over the land.

Some areas are deserts because they are on the sheltered or leeward sides of mountains. The winds bringing moisture from the sea are forced to rise and are cooled when they reach the mountains. The moisture falls as rain on the windward side of the mountains. By the time the winds have passed over the mountains they are dry. This

Coastal desert in Peru

A rare sight: sea fog over the Namib desert in South Africa

happens to the winds which blow over the Great American deserts. We say that the Great American deserts are in a rain shadow.

moist wind | dry wind | dry wind | moist wind

desert

west | east

Atacama desert | Andes | South America

Man-made deserts

Although they are huge, many deserts were in fact man-made. Only 2000 years ago the Thar desert of western India was a forest. There are also many man-made desert areas of Africa. The Romans once cultivated the northern parts of the Sahara.

Often trees were cut down on hills for firewood or to make fields. Ploughing then broke the soil down. Rainwater ran down the slope taking some of the soil with it. Soon the soil was not good enough for crops to grow. It was allowed to grass over and animals were put out to feed. If there were too many animals they destroyed all the plants. All the soil was then washed or blown away leaving bare rock. The once fertile hillside had become a desert.

In many parts of the world sheep or goats are a cause of soil loss. They strip the ground of plants. Rain or wind then removes the soil leaving the ground bare.

But human beings are remarkable creatures. Having made deserts they have also learned how to live in them. In most of the deserts of the world there are people who know how to survive. Desert people can survive in places where most of us would soon die because of the intense heat, or from a lack of water or food.

People can also make deserts

Cutting down forests | Intensive ploughing | Over-grazing | Erosion by wind and rain

Water in the desert

In most deserts some rain does fall occasionally. As we have seen, some deserts may have up to 25 centimetres of rain a year. When the rain comes it is often in a violent thunderstorm. In a few minutes a year's supply of rain can fall. Some of the water quickly evaporates when it touches the hot ground. The water turns into invisible vapour which rises into the air.

Instead of soaking into the ground, much of the water just runs off the hard, dry surface. There may be what is called a 'flash' flood. Then the water rushes down gullies and valleys carrying everything before it. It can carve out deep channels called canyons.

It is very dangerous to camp on the dry bed of a stream in the desert. There could be a flash flood which would sweep away the camp and anyone in it. Soon, however, all desert rivers and streams dry up as the water soaks into the ground. Then everywhere is dry once more.

Rainstorm in Nigeria

A dry river bed or wadi

A 'flash' flood on the Kueseb River in the Namib desert, South Africa

The effects of the desert weather

Eroded rocks in Monument Valley, Arizona, USA

The hot sunshine during the day makes the rocks hot. It makes them so hot that they expand, which means get bigger. At night it is cold so the rocks contract or shrink again. This puts a great strain on the rocks, and pieces of them break off. The rock surface splinters into stones and gravel.

The stones and gravel eventually break down into grains of sand. These materials are blown by the strong winds. The sharp pieces of sand bounce against the rocks. Slowly the rocks are worn away. But sand grains are too heavy for the wind to lift very high. So the wind-blown sand cuts into the rocks nearest the ground. Often the rocks become carved by the wind to look like giant mushrooms. The sand also cuts out caves and arches. The bits of rock form more sand.

In some places the wind blows the sand into great drifts called dunes.

Some sand-dunes are hills more than 300 metres high. Other dunes are shaped like crescents or quarter moons. As the wind blows, the dunes slowly move forward. They may bury villages in their path if nothing is done to stop them.

Some sand-dunes can grow into high hills

Do you remember?

1 What are deserts?

2 What is the most rain, on average, which falls on a desert each year?

3 Where are the cold deserts of the world?

4 On what continents are the hot deserts of the world to be found?

5 What happens in deserts because there are no clouds?

6 What are the three things all plants need in order to grow?

7 How do some desert plants reach the water deep underground?

8 Why do cacti have spines?

9 Where does a cactus store water?

10 Where does the baobab or bottle tree store water?

11 Where do those desert animals which never drink get the water they need to live?

12 Where do many desert animals spend the day? Why?

13 Why do desert animals need good sight and hearing?

14 Why do many desert animals have large ears?

15 Why are the toes of a camel joined together by a fleshy pad?

16 How do camels keep the sand out of their eyes and nostrils?

17 Why do you think camels are better than horses for carrying goods across a desert?

18 How does the Arabian camel or dromedary differ from the bactrian camel?

19 What does the camel store in its hump?

20 Why are some places near the sea deserts?

21 Why do some places that are far from the sea become deserts?

22 What do we mean if we say that somewhere is in a rain shadow?

23 Name two ways in which people have helped to make deserts.

24 What is a canyon?

25 How are canyons formed?

26 Why is it dangerous to camp on the dry bed of a stream in the desert?

27 Why are some rocks in the desert shaped like mushrooms?

28 What is a sand-dune?

29 How has the sand in the desert been formed?

30 What happens when rocks are heated during the day and cooled at night?

Things to do

1 Deserts of the world Find a map of the world. Mount it on a larger sheet of card or wood. Put a pin in each of the world's hot desert areas. Join each pin by a length of thread or cotton to a label on the card or wood stating the name of the desert. Against the label stick a picture showing a typical scene in that desert.

2 Make a wallchart Collect pictures of hot desert scenery. Make a wallchart or scrapbook with your pictures. Write a sentence or two about each of the pictures.

3 Make a simple rain gauge Use a clean washing-up liquid bottle and cut it as shown in the picture. Place the rain gauge in a tray of soil or sand. Stand it out in the open away from trees and buildings. Use the rain gauge to find out how much rain has fallen each day. Measure the depth of water in millimetres.

In a desert, on average, less than 25 centimetres of rain falls each year. This is, on average, less than 5 millimetres of rain a week. How many weeks as dry as that do you experience where you live?

4 Use a thermometer Ask your teacher to let you look at a thermometer. Handle it gently. It will break if you are not careful.

Use your thermometer to find the temperature of things. Try the temperature of the skin of your fingers, water from the tap, some ice or snow, the temperature in the middle of the playground on a sunny day, and under the shade of a tree on the same day, and the temperature of the classroom. Ask your teacher to measure the temperature of boiling water for you.

Take the temperature in the same spot in the playground at the same time every day.

Making a rain gauge

A good time would be 9 o'clock in the morning.

Make a graph showing how the temperature changes from day to day.

Hang a thermometer on a wall outside your classroom. Take the temperature every 30 minutes or every hour throughout one school day.

Make a graph showing how the temperature changes. When is the hottest time of the day and when is it coldest?

In 1922 a temperature of 58°C was recorded in the Libyan Desert. How much hotter is this than the highest temperature you recorded outside your classroom?

5 Find out about evaporation Get two saucers and a small meat-paste jar. Fill the jar to the top with water. Carefully empty this water into one of the saucers. Stand the saucer on a warm windowsill or shelf. Fill the paste jar to the top again with water. Stand it by the side of the saucer of water. What happens to the water after a day or so? Which dries up first? Why? Where has the water gone?

Now use the paste jar to fill two saucers with water. Place one on a sunny windowsill. Put the other somewhere cool, such as on the bottom shelf of a refrigerator. What happens to the water after a day or so? Which dries up first? Why?

6 Wind in the desert In the desert it is often very windy. Does wind make water evaporate faster?

Put the same amount of water in each of two saucers. Stand one saucer outside in the open on a windy day. Place the other saucer in a place outside which is sheltered from the wind.

Look at the two saucers from time to time. From which saucer does the water evaporate fastest? What effect does the wind have on water?

7 Make a collection of sands Sand is made of tiny grains of rock. The colour of sand varies from place to place.

Whenever you go on holiday or on visits to friends or relatives, collect a small sample of the local sand.

Allow the sand to dry and put it in a small clear-glass or plastic bottle of the kind tablets are sold in. Alternatively, you could put the sand in a tall, thin clear-glass bottle. Many wine bottles are ideal. Label each layer of sand with where and when you collected it.

Look at the different samples of sand with a hand lens. What differences do you see?

8 How does sand wear away rocks? It is not easy to see how wind-blown sand wears away rocks. But you can see how sandpaper (which is paper with sand glued on to it) wears away rocks.

Make a collection of small pieces of rock – even pieces of brick and concrete will do. Rub each say 20 times with a piece of the same kind of sandpaper. Which rock shows the most wear? Try other kinds of sandpaper. Do you get the same results?

9 A sandstorm Pretend you are walking across a desert. Suddenly there is a bad sandstorm. Write a story about your adventures.

10 Grow a cactus garden Cacti are not difficult to grow from seeds. You can buy packets of mixed cacti seeds from garden centres.

The seed should be sown during spring or summer. Use well-drained pots or dishes. Put a layer of gravel or pieces of broken clay flowerpot in the bottom of each pot. You can buy special compost; if not, John Innes seed compost will do. The latter is improved if you add a little coarse sand to it.

Sow the seeds on the surface and lightly cover them with silver sand. After sowing, enclose the pot with a polythene bag and shade it with paper until the seedlings appear. It may take a long time (a month or more) for the seeds to grow. Keep the compost moist but not wet.

If the seedlings grow healthily, keep them in pots or dishes for the first year. If they seem unhealthy, then transplant them separately to small pots.

Use a shallow plastic or clay container to make a desert scene with your cacti. Put a layer of gravel or broken flowerpot in the

Making a cactus garden

bottom. Again use compost. To make your desert scene look interesting, include a few stones or pieces of bark.

Cacti need lots of sunshine and warmth. Water them only occasionally or the roots will rot.

11 Inside a cactus If you can obtain a large cactus which is no longer wanted, cut it in half. What is the inside like? Draw the cactus before and after you cut it in half.

12 Collect pictures of desert animals Stick your pictures in a book and write a sentence about each one.

13 Camels and water A camel can drink 115 litres of water or more in one go.

How much water can you drink at one time? Measure it out and see.

How much water and other liquids do you drink in a day? Keep a record and find out. How long would it take you to drink 115 litres?

14 Keeping gerbils Gerbils came originally from the deserts. There they lived in burrows in the ground. Gerbils make good pets and they soon become tame.

You can buy plastic or wire cages for gerbils. Or a large fish tank will do. Cover the floor of the cage with a layer of peat mixed with chopped straw, or with sawdust.

Give the gerbils clean white paper for bedding. They will soon shred it up and

22

make a nest with it.

Put the cage on a shelf or table away from draughts and direct sunlight.

Give your gerbils water in a bottle like that shown in the picture.

Feed your gerbils on a mixture of canary and sunflower seeds, wheat, oats, maize and barley. They also like fresh apple, carrot, or cabbage or lettuce as a treat, and unsugared breakfast cereals.

Gerbils must gnaw a lot or their teeth will grow too long. A dog biscuit can be given to them from time to time. Even better is a small tree branch which they can climb on and gnaw.

Study your gerbils and try to answer these questions about them. You may also think of some questions of your own.

When are gerbils most active?

How often do they eat?

How often do they drink?

What are their favourite foods?

How do gerbils deal with a large piece of food?

How do gerbils clean themselves?

What does a gerbil do if it finds something new in its cage, such as a flowerpot or a cardboard tube?

What noises do gerbils make?

What does a gerbil do if it is frightened?

In what position do gerbils rest or sleep?

Do they sleep and rest in the same spot each day?

Why is it that gerbils do not smell like tame mice or some other pet animals?

How do the bodies of gerbils save water?

15 Pretend that you are a jerboa
You live in a burrow in the sand-dunes in the Sahara desert. You are going out looking for food. Would you be going out looking for food during the day or at night? What other animals might you see? Who or what might you need to hide from? What food would you be looking for? Think about how you would move, and what you would see, hear and smell. Think about how you would feel. Look at the picture below. Write down your story.

16 Why do desert animals often live in burrows? Take two thermometers. On a hot, sunny day, dig a small burrow in the garden. Place one thermometer in the burrow, being careful not to break it. Lay the other thermometer on the surface of the soil. Look at the thermometers from time to time. What differences in temperature do you notice? Can you see why desert animals often spend the day in burrows in the ground?

Things to find out

1 How many continents are there? How many of them have hot deserts?

2 How much rain falls each year, on average, where you live?

3 What are the differences between the temperatures in the sun and in the shade on a hot day?

4 What are days like in this country when there are no clouds? What kind of weather do we get at night in winter when there are no clouds in the sky?

5 Some plants in this country have prickles or thorns like those of desert plants. Find out the names of some of these plants. Which parts of the plants have formed the prickles or thorns? How do the prickles or thorns help the plants?

6 Why is the baobab tree often called the bottle tree?

7 Cacti and other desert plants get much of their water from dew. Many small desert animals lick up the dew. What is dew and how is it formed?

8 The common rabbit was once a desert animal. Find out where it came from and how it got to this country. How could you tell that rabbits came from hot, sandy places?

9 How do large feet help to stop a camel sinking into the sand? Experiment with a tray of sand and large and small model feet made of card, wood or Lego to find out.

10 In 1846, a desert snail was sent from Egypt to the British Museum in London.

The snail was fixed to a card bearing a label. Four years later one of the keepers at the museum saw that the snail was alive. When he gave the snail some cabbage, it came out of its shell and started to crawl about.

Find out how all land snails, including desert snails, are able to survive during long periods of dry weather.

11 Whereabouts, other than in deserts, can you find sand-dunes? How are these sand-dunes formed? What happens to them? What are they sometimes used for?

12 Can you find out where sand is sometimes used to clean buildings? How does the process work? How is it similar to sand blown by the wind against rocks in the desert?

13 What is a mirage? How are mirages formed? Where can you see mirages besides deserts?

Oases

In most parts of the world there is a lot of water under the ground. This is known as the water table. Each time it rains, some of the water is soaked up by the soil. There it is taken up by the roots of plants. Some of the water is carried away by rivers and streams. But a lot of the water eventually seeps down into the ground. It fills all the cracks and openings in the rocks underground. Often it is possible to dig a well to reach this water.

As we have seen, in deserts most of the water from rain is lost. But even under deserts there are underground rivers and streams. Some of these rivers and streams bring their water from mountains hundreds of miles away where there is heavy rainfall or snow. In a few places water from these underground rivers or streams flows to the surface of the desert. The water forms a spring or waterhole. These springs or waterholes in the desert, around which plants can grow, are called oases. A river flowing through a desert may make long oases along its banks.

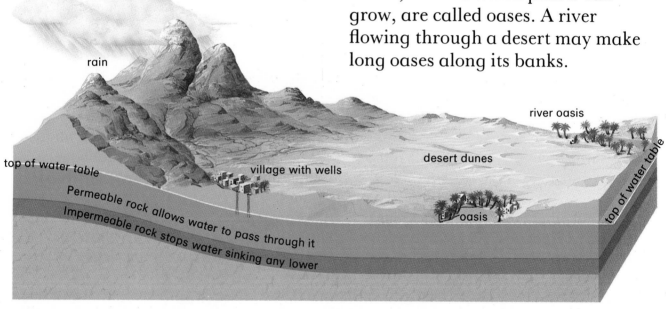

rain

top of water table

Permeable rock allows water to pass through it

Impermeable rock stops water sinking any lower

village with wells

desert dunes

river oasis

oasis

top of water table

Camel helping to pump water from a well

Raising water from a water-hole

26

People in the desert

It is around the oases and water-holes in the desert that towns and villages are built. The people who live in an oasis make use of every centimetre of land. In the oases of the Sahara, they grow food plants such as dates, figs, olives and apricots. They keep cattle, sheep and goats.

People who live in oases are not the only people to live in the desert. Wanderers or nomads also live there. The Bedouin of the Sahara are nomads. They travel from one oasis to another, driving their sheep and goats in front of them. The sheep and goats feed on the scattered desert plants.

Because it is so hot during the day, the Bedouin often travel at night when it is cool. They rest during the daytime. The Bedouin have no fixed homes. They live in tents made from goat skins or camel hair. To protect themselves from the heat, cold, and wind-blown sand, they wear long flowing robes.

Irrigation channels at a Tunisian oasis

Often the Bedouin live only on camel's milk, cheese and dates. For a feast they kill a camel or sheep. The Bedouin have to visit oases to exchange meat and skins for tea, dates, rice and other foods. They also water their camels there.

A Bedouin feast in Saudi Arabia

A Bedouin encampment

27

The Sahara desert

A sandstorm in the Sahara

We have already learned something about the people who live in the Sahara desert. The Sahara is the largest desert in the world. It stretches across Africa from the Atlantic Ocean to the Red Sea. A lot of the Sahara consists of shifting sand-dunes. There are often sandstorms blown up by the strong winds. But there are also plains strewn with gravel and boulders. And there are rocky hills, mountains, and deep gorges.

The Sahara is one of the hottest regions of the world. The hottest months are June, July and August. Then, temperatures of 58°C in the shade have been recorded. Some people still live in caves in the Sahara desert because they are cool. In one part of Tunisia, people have dug caves in the soft rock for themselves and their animals.

Wild animals found in the Sahara include gazelles, oryx, and other antelopes, jackals, foxes and badgers. There used to be lions in the Sahara, but they were all killed off during the last century.

Cave dwellings in Tunisia

Oryx

Date palms

Date palms are the most important plants grown in the oases of the Sahara and Arabian deserts. Dates are brown when ripe. They are food for people and domestic animals. Most of the dates we eat in this country have been dried in the sun.

In the desert oases, date stones are ground up to make camel food. The palm leaves are used as fuel. They can also be used to thatch buildings. The fibres from the dried leaves are twisted into ropes or woven into a coarse cloth, used to make sacks. They can also be used to make brushes. The sap of the tree is used to make wine. Even the trunks of dead palms are used for building houses and fences, so nothing is wasted.

The palm trees provide shade and shelter for other crops. These crops include oranges, figs, olives, apricots, pomegranates, wheat, maize, millet, beans, peas, onions, tobacco and sweet potatoes.

Date palm in bloom

A date palm fence in Algeria

Orange trees growing under date palms in Peru

The Kalahari desert

The red sands of the Kalahari desert

The Kalahari is an inland desert in southern Africa. It is 650 to 800 kilometres across.

Most of the Kalahari desert consists of red sand. This forms long, shifting sand-dunes. Although it is very flat, the Kalahari desert is crossed by ancient dried-up river beds. There are also huge mud flats. When it rains these turn into shallow lakes which may last for several months. They are then visited by thirsty animals.

The Kalahari is called a desert because it is mainly dry, but in places quite a lot of plants grow. The north-west part is covered with dense scrub. There are also tall palms and scattered thorn trees. Watermelons and other plants with long underground stems are common. Many kinds of antelopes and other large animals live in the Kalahari, feeding on the plants that grow there.

The north-west Kalahari scrubland

Grazing Impala

Kalahari Bushmen

The people who live in the Kalahari desert are called Bushmen. They keep no cattle, sheep or goats, but rely on wild animals and plants for food. The Bushmen have excellent eyesight and a keen sense of smell. The men hunt wild animals with spears, clubs and bows. The arrows they use have poisoned tips. Bushmen are very good shots. They can hit a moving antelope with an arrow at a distance of 100 metres. Any meat not eaten by the Bushmen right away is cut into strips and dried in the sun. It is then saved for when food is scarce.

The women and children dig in the earth with sticks, looking for bulbs and roots to eat. Bushmen sometimes get water from underground by using a grass stem to suck it up. They have few possessions. They must travel light in their endless search for food and water. But they do build temporary huts and shelters of branches and grass. They are also famous for their rock paintings.

Kalahari Bushmen dividing the catch

Bushmen huts

Rock paintings in the Tsoldilo Hills of Botswana, Africa

The Australian desert

A red kangaroo

Ayer's Rock in central Australia

The mining town of Kalgoorlie

Most of the central part of Australia is a desert. It is over 1500 kilometres across. There is a vast area of red sand. There are also spiny bushes and salt lakes. Because of the dryness of the climate, bush fires are common; but seeds of many of the plants are able to survive the fire. And some of them will not start to grow unless fire has passed over them.

The animals of the Australian desert are very interesting because they are found nowhere else in the world. They include kangaroos and wallabies. Their newborn are very tiny and undeveloped. They are carried in a pouch on the mother's belly until they are large enough to fend for themselves. Pouched animals are called marsupials.

In the middle of the Australian desert there are some towns. Norseman and Kalgoorlie, for instance, were built because gold was discovered nearby. More recently the metal nickel has been mined there. The people in these towns get their water from Perth 564 kilometres away. It is carried to these and other desert towns in large pipelines.

32

Australian Aborigines

Before white people went to live in Australia, only the Aborigines lived in the Australian desert. They survived because they knew all about the animals and plants in the desert. They knew where water was to be found.

Today most Aborigines work on farms or in cities. Only a few tribes still roam the Australian deserts. Like the Kalahari Bushmen, these Aborigines have few possessions. They hunt animals with spears and boomerangs, or gather roots, bulbs and grubs to eat. The Aborigines are experts at tracking animals. They wear few clothes but their dark skins protect them from the sun's rays. Their only shelter is a crude hut or windbreak of sticks and grass called a wurlie. The Aborigines can make fires by rubbing sticks together.

A kill of kangaroo

An Aboriginal dwelling

Some Aborigines work on farms

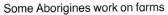

The Atacama desert

In northern Chile is the Atacama desert. It is a vast strip of dry barren land. It stretches for 970 kilometres. Parts of the Atacama are very cold because they are a long way above sea-level. The Atacama is the world's driest desert. This is because the winds blow off the land towards the sea all the year round. There is one desert weather station at which no rain has ever been recorded. In the whole length of the Atacama there is only one river.

Until fairly recently, the only people who lived in the Atacama were people called Indians. They lived in rough stone huts. The Indians depended on the llama, a relative of the camel. They used the llama to carry them and their possessions. They made warm clothing from the llama's wool. The llama also provided meat.

Today not many Indians live in the higher parts of the Atacama. This is because the desert has a huge supply

A sodium nitrate mine

of a substance called sodium nitrate. Sodium nitrate is mined for use as a fertilizer. The world's largest copper mine is also found in the Atacama. So nowadays most Indians work in the mines and live in the mining towns and villages.

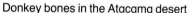
Donkey bones in the Atacama desert

Herding llamas by Lake Titicaca, Peru

The Gobi desert

The Gobi desert has hot summers. But the winters are very cold because the Gobi is situated on high ground far from the Equator in central Asia. There are high mountains in the Gobi. Trees are almost unknown. The only plants are wind-swept grasses, thorn bushes and patches of scrub. Water is found only at wells or in the occasional salty lake.

The commonest wild animal in the Gobi is the long-tailed gazelle. There are many kinds of eagles, hawks and vultures. Snakes, lizards and other reptiles are rare because they cannot survive the cold winters. But fossil eggs of dinosaurs have been found in the Gobi desert. This shows that these giant reptiles were once able to survive there.

The people of the Gobi are the

Yaks in the snow

Mongols. They ride short-legged furry horses. They farm herds of yaks. The yak is a relative of domestic cattle. The Mongol people live in tents called yurts. These are made of fur, felt and animals' skins stretched over poles.

A yurt encampment in winter

Vulture surveying the desert

The Great American desert

The sand-dunes of the Great American desert are smaller than those of the Sahara. But there are many more rocky mountain slopes, and boulder-strewn valleys and canyons. Many of the rocks are beautiful colours. They have been carved into fantastic shapes by the wind.

Summers in the Great American desert are extremely hot, but winters are cool or even cold. Dense scrub grows in parts of the desert. There are also many cacti. One of the commonest bushes is the creosote bush. The roots of this bush produce a chemical which passes into the soil. This stops other plants from growing nearby so that they do not take the water the creosote bush needs.

American deserts are home to a number of interesting animals. They include the jaguar, puma, peccary, prong-horned antelope and bighorn sheep. The Great American desert is not as big as it used to be. This is because the government has built dams across some of the big rivers that cross it. Water is stored behind the dams. Some of this water is used to make crops grow in the desert.

The Grand Canyon, Arizona, USA

A creosote bush

The collared peccary

The desert long ago

Some deserts have not always been dry and bare. Thousands of years ago the land that is now the Sahara desert was lush and green. Many people lived there. They kept large herds of sheep, cattle and goats. They hunted wild animals for food, and caught fish.

Paintings on the walls of caves in the middle of what is now the Sahara show us that it was once a fertile land. There were flowing rivers where crocodiles and hippopotamuses swam. Elephants, lions, giraffes, ostriches and other animals were common. And then, about 3000 years ago the climate changed, and the heavy rain stopped. The land began

An ancient Saharan cave painting shows which animals once lived there

to dry out. The grass no longer grew so well. The sheep, cattle and goats ate away a lot of the remaining grass leaving bare ground. The fertile soil blew away, leaving only sand and bare rocks.

The Sahara desert as it might have looked 3,000 years ago

Wealth in the desert

Until fairly recently harsh barren deserts were almost useless to people. People who lived there were usually poor and had to struggle to survive.

But a number of valuable minerals have been found. Gold, uranium, and aluminium ore have been discovered in the Australian desert. Copper and sodium nitrate are mined in the Atacama. Diamonds are mined in the Namib desert in Southern Africa. Oil and natural gas have been found in large quantities under the Sahara, Arabian and Great American deserts. Several desert countries have now become very rich from the money they receive for this oil and gas. New cities, roads, railways and airports have been built with this money. Now cars, lorries, trains and aircraft have often replaced the camels.

In addition, many tourists now visit deserts for their holidays. The money tourists spend helps the desert people to buy the things they need.

A diamond mine in the Namib desert, South Africa

An oil refinery in Algeria

The Pan-American highway, Peru

Jeddah: a modern desert city

Planting the desert

An irrigation canal in Mongolia

Reclaiming the Gobi desert with a 'green wall' of trees

Tomato fields in the Negev desert, Israel

If water can be brought to the deserts then crops can be grown. Water can be brought from wells and rivers to put on the dry land. This watering is called irrigation.

Some of the richest farmland in the United States of America is in southern California. Huge crops of fruit and vegetables are grown all the year round. Yet only a few years ago this was dry desert. The change was brought about when water from the Colorado River was used to irrigate the land. In Israel, large areas of the Negev desert are being used to grow crops such as tomatoes, avocados and oranges. Again this has been done with the help of irrigation. However, it is not always easy to make deserts fertile by irrigation. Much water under the Sahara desert is too salty for most plants to grow in it.

It is possible to stop the desert sand blowing about by spraying the dunes with a mixture of oil and rubber. This mixture also stops the sand from drying out. Then seedlings of acacia or eucalyptus trees are planted. The tree roots bind the sand to stop it from blowing away. Other plants such as date palms and orange trees are then able to grow in their shade and shelter.

Do you remember?

1 What is the water table?

2 How can we reach the water table?

3 What do we call springs and waterholes in the desert?

4 Whereabouts in the desert are towns and villages built?

5 What are nomads?

6 What do Bedouin live in?

7 What kinds of animals do the Bedouin keep?

8 Which is the largest hot desert in the world?

9 Why do some people in Tunisia live in caves?

10 Name four things which date palms are used for.

11 How do date palms help other crops?

12 Name another desert, besides the Sahara, which is found in Africa.

13 What do the Bushmen use when hunting?

14 How do the Bushmen obtain water to drink?

15 Where do the Bushmen make their paintings?

16 What are marsupials and where are they found?

17 Name two kinds of marsupial.

18 Where do most Australian Aborigines now live and work?

19 What did the Aborigines use for hunting?

20 How did the Aborigines make fire?

21 What are the people called who live in the Atacama desert?

22 What substances are mined in the Atacama desert?

23 What are the people called who live in the Gobi desert?

24 What is unusual about the creosote bush?

25 Why is the Great American desert not as big as it used to be?

26 What was the Sahara desert like long ago?

27 Name four valuable minerals found in deserts.

28 What has made several desert countries rich?

29 What is irrigation?

30 What is being done to stop the desert sand from blowing away?

Things to do

1 A journey across the Sahara desert

Imagine you are going to travel across the Sahara desert on a camel train. Look at an atlas and decide where you are going to travel from and where you are going to. Write a story about your journey and the adventures you have. What will you eat on your journey and where will you find water? Where will you sleep at night?

2 Building a solar still

Although it rarely rains in the desert, there is often water in the soil.

Desert travellers can get water to drink by making a solar still. The only equipment they need is a sheet of polythene and a jar or tin to collect the water. You can make a solar still in hot weather on a beach or in the garden to see how it works.

Dig a hole at least 1 metre across and 60 centimetres deep. Put the tin or jar in the centre.

Spread the sheet of polythene over the hole. Fix the edges with stones. Place a flat stone in the centre of the polythene so that it sags towards the tin or jar. The polythene should not touch the soil.

Then sit and wait for water to collect in the tin or jar. The sun heats the soil beneath the polythene. Moisture condenses on the underside of the polythene and drips down into the tin or jar. How long does it take for the tin or jar to fill with water?

3 Cleaning dirty water

Every drop of water in the desert is precious, even dirty water. Can we make dirty water clean?

You will need some clean jam-jars; a clean flowerpot; a sheet of paper; cotton wool; some clean, washed sand and gravel; some soil.

Shake some soil in a jar with water to make the water muddy.

A solar still
Making a solar still

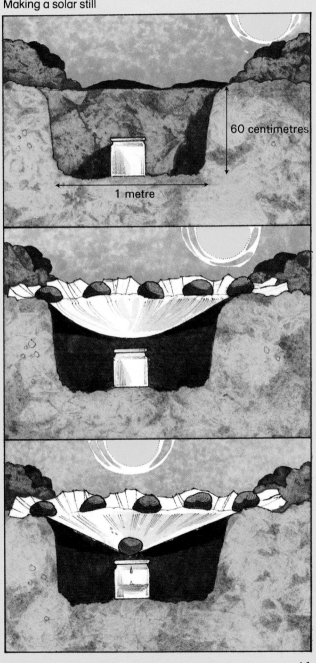

60 centimetres

1 metre

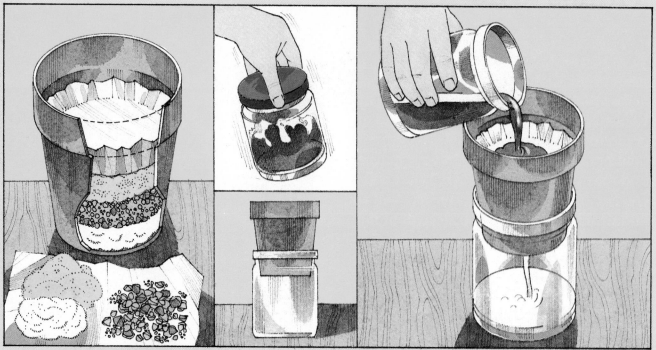

Put a layer of cotton wool in the bottom of the flowerpot. On top of this put a layer of clean gravel about 3 or 4 centimetres thick. Cover the gravel with a layer of clean sand about 3 or 4 centimetres thick. Lay a piece of paper on top of the sand. Stand the flowerpot on top of a clean jar, so that the drainage holes are over the jar.

Carefully pour the muddy water on to the piece of paper in the flowerpot.

What is the water like which comes out of the flowerpot into the jar at the bottom? Is it still muddy? Is it fit to drink?

Our flowerpot acts as a filter. It filters or sieves the soil out of the water. Where else is a filter used to clean dirty water? How is water made pure for drinking?

Can you use your flowerpot filter to get the salt out of salty water?

4 Make a model palm tree Take a sheet of thick paper and roll it into a cylinder. Stick the ends with glue or Sellotape. Cut the palm tree leaves as shown in the picture. Colour your palm tree with paint, felt-tipped pens or crayons. Use a piece of clay or plasticine to help your palm tree to stand up.

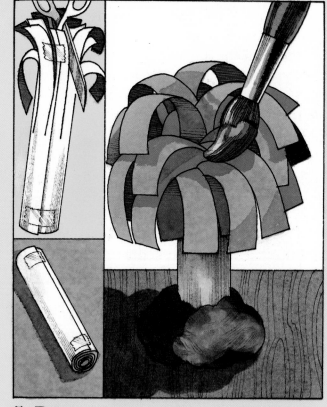

5 Dates Collect the labels off packets or cartons which contained dates. Mount these labels on a sheet of card or in a scrapbook. Which countries did the dates come from?

Can you find the labels of any other foods which came from desert areas?

6 Date and walnut cake Dates are grown in many oases in the Sahara desert. Here is a delicious cake you can make using dates.

You will need:
200g of self-raising flour
100g of margarine or cooking fat
100g of sugar
50g of walnuts
150g of stoned dates
1 egg
approximately 75 millilitres of milk

Ask a grown-up to help you.

1　Use a knife to chop the dates and walnuts into small pieces.
2　Sieve the flour into a mixing bowl. Then rub in the margarine or cooking fat until the mixture looks like fine breadcrumbs.
3　Add the sugar, chopped walnuts, egg and milk to the flour and margarine mixture. Stir the mixture with a wooden spoon until it is well mixed and forms a ball.
4　Grease and flour the inside of a 1kg loaf tin. Put in the mixture and flatten the top.
5　Bake the cake in a moderately hot oven (180°C, 350°F, Gas mark 4), for about 1 to 1¼ hours. The cake should be nicely risen and firm to the touch. (Ask a grown-up to tell you when the cake is cooked and to take it out of the oven for you).
6　When the cake is cool, turn it out of the loaf tin.

This cake tastes particularly good cut in slices and spread with butter.

7 Growing dates and orange pips

Two plants grown in desert oases are date palms and orange trees.

You can grow your own date palms or orange trees. All you need are some small plant pots, polythene bags, and some seed compost or rich garden soil. You also need some date stones and orange pips (or you could use the pips of lemons, tangerines or grapefruit).

Fill the pots to within 1 centimetre of the top with compost. Sow the date stones 2 or 3 centimetres deep.

Soak the pots by standing them up to their rims in water. Let them drain, and enclose each one in a polythene bag. Seal each bag with a rubber band.

Stand the pots somewhere warm – a corner of the airing cupboard or on a shelf near a radiator is ideal.

As soon as a seedling appears in each pot, move it onto a sunny windowsill. Remove the polythene bag. Keep the plants out of draughts. After a few months repot them singly in new soil or potting compost. See that the compost stays moist by careful watering.

8 Make a model water table and well

You will need an aquarium or washing up bowl, some sand, and a plastic tube, or a plastic bottle with the top and bottom cut off.

Stand the tube up in the bowl or aquarium. Build a hill of gravel around it, as shown in the picture. Pour a little water into the bowl or aquarium. Measure how deep it is with a ruler. How deep is the water in your well? Is the water deeper in the well?

Where would be the best place to dig a well on the slope of a hill? Would it be near the top of the hill or near the bottom? Why?

9 Make a model oasis

Make a model oasis in a large tray. Use sand and papier mâché to make the hills, rocks and sand-dunes. Paint a piece of paper blue to represent a water-hole. Make small palm trees from paper as described on page 42. Make model houses from matchboxes.

10 How does the kind of soil affect the way in which plants grow?

One problem with growing plants in the desert is the lack of water. But how will seeds grow in sand if they are watered?

You will need some good garden soil or seed compost, some sand, and some small flowerpots or clean yoghurt pots.

Fill one pot with soil. Fill another with sand. Sprinkle cress seeds on to the soil and sand. Gently press the seeds into the soil and sand with your fingers or with a small piece of flat wood.

Stand the pots on a sunny windowsill.

Keep both pots watered regularly, using the same amount of water for each pot. In which pot do the cress seeds grow best? Or are there no differences?

Try this experiment now with other kinds of seeds: lettuce and radish seeds would be good ones to start with. What differences do you see? What causes them?

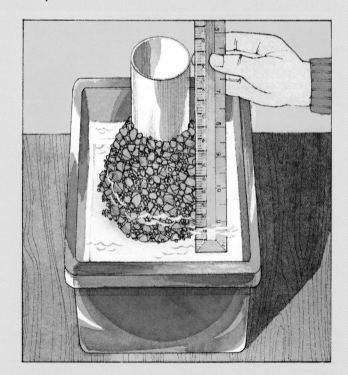

11 How do different colours absorb the sun's rays?

You will need two similar thermometers and some sheets of paper all the same size but of different colours.

Lay the two thermometers next to each other in sunshine. What is the temperature?

Cover one thermometer with a sheet of black paper and the other with a sheet of white paper. Leave them in the sunshine for 15 to 30 minutes. Now quickly remove the two sheets of paper. What temperature does each of the two thermometers say? Under which sheet of paper was it hotter? Under which sheet of paper was it cooler? Which colour paper absorbs more of the sun's rays?

Now try the experiment with sheets of paper of other colours. Try the experiment with different coloured pieces of cloth.

What colour clothes would it be best to wear if you were cold? What colour clothes would you wear if you were going out in a hot desert?

If you cannot do this experiment in sunshine, you can always do it using the light and heat from a table lamp. See that the light falls equally on both sheets of paper, though.

12 Make a model boomerang

It is not easy to make a boomerang like the ones the Aborigines use. This model boomerang is easier to make. It works in the same kind of way.

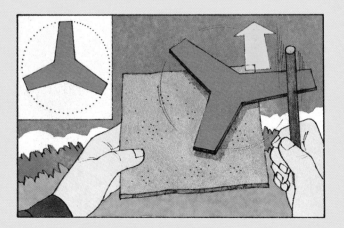

Cut the shape shown in the picture out of thick card. Rest the boomerang on the edge of a large square of card or hardboard. Hold the card or hardboard in one hand.

Hit the overhanging arm of the boomerang sharply with a stick. The boomerang should fly off, loop and return. It if does not, then keep trying. You will soon learn how to do it properly.

13 A model Bushman's shelter

Use twigs, drinking straws and dried grass to make a model of a Bushman's shelter. If you are able to, in summer, make a full-size model of a Bushman's shelter using branches, grasses and bracken.

Imagine you had to sleep under your shelter at night in the Kalahari desert. Write a story describing what you might see, hear and feel during the night.

14 A shaduf

In the oases by the River Nile, water is still often brought up from wells by means of a shaduf, like that in the picture.

Use Meccano or wood to make a model shaduf. How does the shaduf make the work of lifting water easier? Why does it have a weight at one end? Why is the shaduf not pivoted in the middle?

15 A desert frieze

Make a desert frieze to go round the wall of your classroom. Include in your frieze sand-dunes and other desert scenes, camels, Bedouin and their tents, sheep and goats, and an oasis.

Things to find out

1 Look at an atlas. Which continent do you think has the greatest total area of desert on it?

2 What happens to our bodies when we are too hot? What sorts of things can we do to help cool ourselves down?

3 What is an artesian well? Where is it made? What is it used for?

4 What are the desert places people most often visit during their holidays? Look at travel agents' advertisements and brochures to find out. What are the attractions of these places to holiday-makers?

5 What kinds of clothes do people wear in the desert? What colours are they? What materials are the clothes made from? Collect pictures of the different kinds of clothes desert people wear.

6 Find out about the kinds of homes people have in different desert areas. What are these homes made of? Why are so many houses in desert areas painted white? Why do they often have thick walls and small windows? Collect pictures of the different kinds of houses and make a wallchart of them.

7 What other animals besides camels and yaks do people use to carry them and their belongings across the desert? How are these animals adapted to this kind of work?

8 What else are camels used for besides carrying people and their belongings?

9 The Tuareg are a group of people who live in the desert. Find out exactly

whereabouts the Tuareg live. What kinds of homes do they have? How do they travel from place to place? What do they eat? What kinds of clothes do they wear? What kinds of animals do they keep?

10 Use an atlas to find out roughly what proportion of Australia is desert. Can you find a more accurate way of judging how much of Australia is desert?

11 What is humus? What does it do to the soil? Why is there so little humus in desert soils?

12 Use an atlas to find a road or railway which crosses a large desert. How long is the road or railway? What places does it join? Pretend you travelled across the desert between these places by train or Landrover. Describe your journey.

Glossary

Here are the meanings of some words which you might have met for the first time in this book.

Adapted: the ways in which plants and animals (including people) are suited to living in certain conditions.

Cactus: a plant with thick fleshy stems and spiny leaves which is adapted to growing in very dry conditions.

Canyon: a large deep valley with steep sides.

Contract: when somethings gets smaller as it is cooled, it contracts.

Dam: a large wall or bank built to hold back water and raise its level. A large lake called a reservoir is often formed behind the dam.

Desert: a dry region of the world in which few plants are able to grow.

Equator: an imaginary circle around the centre of the Earth which is an equal distance from the North and South Poles.

Evaporate: when water is heated it disappears into the air as water vapour. We say the water has evaporated.

Expand: when something gets bigger as it is heated, it expands.

Fertile: a good soil which grows many plants is said to be fertile.

Flash flood: after a sudden rainstorm, water may rush down the beds of rivers causing what is called a flash flood.

Gorge: a deep narrow valley.

Irrigation: watering the land by artificial means so that crops will grow.

Leeward: the sheltered side of a hill or mountain.

Marsupials: animals whose babies are born very early in their development. The baby marsupial is then carried around in a pouch on its mother's body until it is large enough to fend for itself.

Minerals: the chemical substances which make up rocks.

Nomads: people who roam from place to place looking for food for their animals, instead of living in a permanent home.

Oasis: a fertile place in a desert where water is available. (The plural of oasis is oases.)

Ore: a solid mixture of rock and minerals, dug from the ground, in which metals and valuable things may be found.

Rain shadow: an area on the sheltered or leeward side of mountains where there is usually less rainfall than on the other, windward, side.

Sand-dune: a hill or ridge of loose sand which has been blown into drifts by the wind.

Spring: a flow of water from the ground. Many streams and rivers start off as springs.

Tourists: people who travel from place to place during their holidays.

Water vapour: the invisible gas which is formed when water is heated.

Well: a deep hole in the ground through which water or oil can be brought to the surface.

Windward: the side of a hill facing the wind.

Index

A
Aborigines *33*
acacia 7, 39
adaptation 7
Africa 5, 7, 12, 14–16, 28–29, 31, 38
air 7, 11, 13
airports 38
Algeria 5, 29, 38
America (see U.S.A.)
animals 8–10, 15, 28–33, 37
Antarctic 4
antelopes 28, 30–31, 36
apricots 29
Arabian camel (see camel)
Arabian desert 29, 38
arches 17
Arctic 4
Arizona 8, 17, 36
arrows 31
Asia 5, 12
Atacama desert 14, 34, 38
Atlantic ocean 28
Australia 5, 8, 32–33
Australian desert 32, *38*
Ayer's Rock 32

B
bactrian (see camel)
badgers 8
baobabs 8
beans 29
Bedouin 27
boomerang 33, 45
Botswana 31
bottle trees (see baobabs)
boulders 28
brushes 29
bulbs 31–32
burrows 9–10, 24
bushes 32, 35
Bushmen *31*, 35

C
cacti 8, 21–22, 36
California 7, 9, 39
camel *11–12*, 22, 26, 29
camel train 11
camping 16
canyons 16, 36
caravan 11
cattle 35, 37
caves 17, 28, 37
Chile 34
China 9
Colorado 39
contraction 16
copper 34, 38
creosote bush 36
crocodiles 37
crops 15, 29, 36, 39
cultivation 5

D
dams 36
dates 27, 29, 43–44
Death Valley 7
dew 8, 25
diamonds 38
dinosaurs 35
dromedary (see camel)
dunes 5, 17, 28, 36

E
eagles 35
elephants 8, 37
Equator 13, 35
erosion 15
eucalyptus 39
evaporation 7, 8, 16, 20
expansion 16

F
felt 35
fertility 15, 37
fertilizer 34
fibre 29
fields 15
figs 27, 29
fire 32, 33
firewood 15
fish 37
flash flood 16
flowers 7
food 29, 31
forests 14
fossils 35
foxes 10, 28
fruit 39
fuel 39
fur 11, 35

G
gas 38
gazelles 28, 35
gecko 9
gerbil 9, 22
giraffes 37
goats 15, 27, 37
Gobi desert 14, 35, 39
gold 32, 38
gorges 28
Grand Canyon 36
graph 20
grasses 15, 34, 37
gravel 16, 17, 28
grazing 15, 30
Great American desert 14, 36, 38
Greenland 4
grubs 33
gullies 16, 36

H
hares 11
hawks 35
hearing 10
heat 6, 10, 28
hides 11
hills 15, 28, 38
hippopotamus 37
humps 11–12
humus 46
hunting 31
huts 31, 34

I
ice 4
impala 30
India 11, 15
Indians (S. American) 34
insects 10
irrigation 39
Israel 39

J
jackals 28
jaguar 36
Jeddah 38
jerboa 9, 24
jungle 15

K
Kalahari desert 8, 30, 31
Kalgoorlie 32
kangaroos 32
Kueseb river 16

L
lakes 5, 13, 30, 32, 34, 35
Libya 6
lions 28, 37
lizards 35
llamas 34

M
maize 29
marsupials 32
mesquite tree 7
Middle East 11
millet 29
minerals 38
mining 32, 34
mirage 25
moisture 13, 14
Mongolia 9, 39
Mongols 35
Monument Valley 17
mountains 5, 14, 28
mud flats 30

N
Namib desert 14, 16, 38
Negev desert 39
nickel 32
Nigeria 16
night 6, 8, 9, 10, 27
Nile 45
Norseman 32
nomads 27

O
oasis (*plural*: oases) 26–27, 29, 39, 44
oil 38–39
olives 27, 29
oranges 29, 44
oryx 28
ostriches 37

P
paintings, (rock) 31, 37
palms 29, 30, 42
Pan-American highway 38
peas 29
peccary 36
Peru 14, 29, 34, 38
pipelines 32
plants 10, 15, 27, 30–32
planting 38
ploughing 15
poison 31
poles 35
pomegranates 29
prickly pear 8
puma 36

R
rabbits 25
railways 38
rain 4–6, 8, 13–16
rain gauge 9
rain shadow 14
rats, (desert) 9
rays 45
Red Sea 28
reptiles 35
rice 27
rivers 13, 16, 26, 37
river beds 16, 30
roads 38
Romans 15
roots 7–8, 26, 31–32, 39
ropes 29

rubber 39

S
Sahara desert 9–10, 15, *28*, 29, 36–39, 41
salt 5
sandpaper 21
sandstorm 21, 28
sap 29
Saudi Arabia 27
scorpion 10
scrubland 30, 34, 36
seedlings 39
seeds 7, 32
shaduf 45
sheep 15, 27
sight 10
snakes 35
snow 4
sodium nitrate 34, 38
soil 15, 26, 54
solar still 41
South America 5, 14
spears 31
spines 8
springs 26
stem 8
stings 10
stones 16
storms 4, 16
streams 16, 26
sweet potatoes 29

T
temperature 19, 28
tents 35
Thar desert 15
thatch 29
thermometer 19
Titicaca, Lake 34
tobacco 29
tomatoes 39
tourism 38, 46
tracking 33
transport 38
trunks 29
Tsoldilo Hills 31
Tuaregs 46
Tunisia 4, 27, 28

U
United States of America 5, 7–8, 10, 14, 17, 35–36, 39

V
valleys 16–17, 36
vegetables 39
vultures 35

W
wadi 46
wallabies 32
walnut cake 43
water 7–9, 12, *16*, 31–32, 36, 41
waterholes 26–27
watermelons 30
water table 26, 44
water vapour 13
wealth *38*
weather station 33
weaving 29
wells 26–27, 35, 38, 44, 46
wheat 29
wind 5, 13–15, 17, 33, 36
wine 29
wool 34

Y
yaks 35
yurts 35